CONTENTS

INTRODUCTION

Everyone in the world experiences hunger. For most of us it is a slightly uncomfortable feeling, an emptiness in the stomach just before we sit down for our next meal. We put up with this feeling because we know that the next meal is on its way. But for more than 750 million people the next meal may not be served.

These 750 million people cannot rely on regular meals. They are lucky if they eat one meal a day. Some of them eat only once or twice a week. They are always hungry. For many of them, their hunger is so great that they die of starvation. More than 10,000 of them die *every day*. Many of the starving live in parts of the world affected by famine. Famine is the complete absence of food. This may be caused by the failure of the crops. In some places it is caused by the failure to move the harvest to where the starving people are dying.

Hungry people are found in every country in the world. They are the poorest and the most neglected people in their country. In the USA most of the people are well fed. But there are eight million adults and 12 million children who do not get enough to eat – one person in every 100 in the USA is hungry. Most of them live in the slums of great cities such as New York and New Orleans.

In some poorer countries the situation is very much worse. In Ethiopia only about one person

In some communities (below left: Leh-Ladakh, India) animals are vital for survival.
This malnourished refugee child in Mali, Africa (below), is being fed a special porridge.

Smokey Mountain Slum in Manila, in the Philippines, is built on a rubbish tip. Millions of people live in similar conditions.

in every 100 has enough to eat. Most of the people in Ethiopia are hungry, and many of them are starving to death.

Countries such as the USA are called developed countries. In the developed countries there is some hunger but very little starvation. On the other hand Ethiopia is a developing country. In some developing countries there is a lot of hunger. Many of the hungry receive no help and begin to starve.

Hungry people do not have a good balanced diet. Their small amounts of food do not have the variety needed to keep them healthy. They often suffer from malnutrition, which literally means 'bad feeding'. This means not just that there is not enough food but also that the food may be of such poor quality as to be unhealthy. As a result, the hungry people of the world are also the sick people of the world (see page 10). They are often too ill to work hard. Just looking after themselves properly is difficult. The weakest of them soon die. Small babies are most at risk. Their mothers may be too ill to look after

them properly and to feed them. So the babies are born into a world of starvation, and many die. One of the main differences between the rich developed countries and the poor developing countries is the number of babies that die before they are one year old (see page 8).

People in developed countries can also suffer from malnutrition. Overeating and eating too many sweet foods can cause malnutrition. In the USA and some western European countries it is estimated that for every person suffering from hunger there are three people suffering from overeating and being overweight. The difference between the greedy and the hungry is that the hungry have no choice.

This book is mainly about the hungry and the starving peoples of the world. But it is also about the rest of us: the well-fed people of the world. What can we do to help the people who are always hungry? Are we doing enough to help the victims of famine? Do other people go hungry because of the way we live? These questions are discussed in this book.

CHAPTER ONE

WHO ARE THE HUNGRY?

Hunger in history

The problems of hunger and famine are not new. One of the earliest recorded examples of famine – in about 1870 BC – is found in the Bible, in the Book of Genesis:

'And there was a famine in the land, and Abram went down into Egypt to sojourn there; for the famine was grievous in the land.'

The farmers in ancient Egypt grew their crops, mainly grain crops, on the floodplains of the River Nile. In years of drought the River Nile was very low and the crops were destroyed by lack of water.

Crop failures may also be caused partly by pests and diseases. In Ireland in 1845, the potato crop was destroyed by a fungus. Potatoes were the main food for most people in Ireland, and by 1850 about one and a half million people had died of starvation. About the same number of people emigrated to America, Canada and England during the famine years, in the hope of finding a better life.

Some countries are repeatedly hit by floods and have a terrible history of famine and suffering. Bangladesh (originally named Bengal) is such a country. In 1991 Bangladesh was devastated by a cyclone. More than a quarter of a million people died by drowning, starvation or disease. In 1942 a general famine began to

This picture captures the despair of refugees from drought in a camp in Ethiopia, Africa.

REPAIRING THE DAMAGE
Famine *and* Hunger

Lawrence Williams

Cloverleaf
An imprint of Evans Brothers Limited

Cloverleaf is an imprint of Evans Brothers Limited

Evans Brothers Limited
2A Portman Mansions
Chiltern Street
London W1M 1LE

First published 1992
Reprinted 1993

For Oxfam in admiration

Typeset by Fleetlines Typesetters, Southend-on-Sea
Printed in Spain by GRAFO, S.A. – Bilbao

ISBN 0 237 51211 4

Acknowledgements

Editor: Su Swallow
Design: Neil Sayer
Production: Jenny Mulvanny

Maps: Hardlines, Charlbury
Illustrations: Jillian Luff of Bitmap Graphics

For permission to reproduce copyright material the author and
publishers gratefully acknowledge the following:

Cover (boy carrying foreign aid bread in Mauritania, Sahel,
Africa) Steve McCurry, Magnum
Title page (Refugee camp in Senegal) Jeremy Hartley, Panos
Pictures
p4 (left) Robert Harding Picture Library, (right) Jeremy
Hartley, Panos Pictures **p5** Michael MacIntyre, Hutchison
Library **p6** Hutchison Library **p8** Vadim Krohin, Hutchison
Library **p9** Sarah Errington, Hutchison Library **p10** Barbara
Klass, Panos Pictures **p11** Luiz Claudio Marigo, Bruce Coleman
Limited **p12** Trygve Bølstad, Panos Pictures **p14** eyewitness
account taken from an article in The Observer Newspaper
24.3.91, (left) Edward Parker, Hutchison Library, (right) Trygve
Bølstad, Panos Pictures **p15** Ian Berry, Magnum, (inset)
Hutchison Library **p16** Hutchison Library **p17** (top) K Helbig,
ZEFA, (bottom) Charlie Ott, Bruce Coleman Limited **p18**
Robert Harding Picture Library **p19** Richard Anthony, Holt
Studios Ltd **p22** (left) Sarah Errington, Hutchison Library,
(right) Christine Pemberton, Hutchison Library **p23** J Holmes,
Panos Pictures **p24** Konrad Wothe, Bruce Coleman Limited
p25 (top) Ron Giling, Panos Pictures, (bottom) Holt Studios
p26 Hutchison Library **p27** (top) Ian Berry, Magnum, (bottom)
Hutchison Library **p28** Betty Press, Panos Pictures **p29** Sarah
Errington, Hutchison Library **p30** M Franck, Magnum **p31** Liba
Taylor, Hutchison Library **p32** (top) Harald Lange, Bruce
Coleman Limited, (bottom) G Ziesler, ZEFA **p34** Karen
Twining/Oxfam **p35** Sarah Errington, Hutchison Library **p37**
Gryniewicz/ ECOSCENE **p39** J Hartley, Panos Pictures **p40**
(top left) G and P Corrigan, Robert Harding Picture Library,
(top right) Zachmann, Magnum, (bottom left) G and P Corrigan,
Robert Harding Picture Library, (bottom right) Norman
Tomalin, Bruce Coleman Limited **p41** Nicholas Devore, Bruce
Coleman Limited **p42** (top) B Barbey, Magnum, (bottom) Peter
Marlow, Magnum **p43** Ron Giling, Panos Pictures

develop after another cyclone had struck. By 1946 more than three million people had died. In a report to the Bengal Relief Committee, a headmaster in Dacca wrote:

'The sufferings of the people cannot even be imagined. The whole population seems to be moving silently towards death. Men have neither the capacity nor the energy even to try to live. A stupor seems to have overtaken all. The poorer section, I mean the free-kitchen goers, are dying of fasting and cold. When they find they cannot walk to the kitchen they lie about it on the cold ground under the winter sky and without any clothes. But death soon relieves them of all their sufferings. The middle class gentry have not that advantage also. They cannot get the gruel from a free kitchen. They can only starve themselves to death, silently at home. All sorts of corruption are running rampant.
Free kitchens have been started in many villages. The Government supplies the ration. But some unscrupulous persons are making a profit of it. The *khichuri* [gruel mixture] may be sold in the black market. Needy and greedy persons have got into the union food committees, and the food-grains supplied are not properly distributed.'

Two centuries earlier, the country suffered a similar tragedy, this time caused by droughts. An employee of the East India Company wrote in a letter in 1770:

'How shall I describe the misery of the country from the excessive droughts, the dearness and scarcity of grain hitherto, but now a total failure? The tanks and springs are dried up, and water grows daily more difficult to be procured. Added to these calamities, frequent and dreadful fires have happened throughout the country, impoverished whole families, and destroyed thousands of lives . . . Some hopes were still left that during the months of April and May we should be blessed with rain, and the poor *ryots* [peasant farmers] able to till their ground; but to this hour not a drop has fallen. The coarse crop which is gathered at this season is entirely spoilt, and the seed for the August crop is sown during the months of April and May. It is now the middle of the latter month, and they have not begun for want of rain. Even now, by the help of a few showers, something might be done. If the scarcity of grain and want of rain had been confined to one spot in the province, management and attention might find a remedy; but when the evil is total, there can be no remedy but in the mercy of God.'

How many worlds?

The countries of the world are often divided into two groups: the rich, developed countries and the poorer, developing countries.

The developed countries are sometimes called First World countries. They include the USA, Great Britain, France and Japan. These countries can feed their own people from what they can grow at home plus what they can afford to buy from other countries. They have surpluses of food, which they can store or sell. Less than a third of the world's population lives in developed countries.

The poorer developing countries contain more than two thirds of the world's population. A few of these countries have succeeded in developing, often with the help of skills and money from developed countries. These Second World countries include Argentina, Portugal, Egypt, parts of Brazil and oil-rich countries in the Middle East.

In many other very poor countries, western-style development is either not succeeding or is making the people even poorer and hungrier. These countries are known as the Third World countries. They include Ethiopia and the Sudan in Africa, and Bangladesh and Cambodia in Asia.

It seems that as the rich get richer the poor do get poorer. Is it not time to speak of living together in one world?

So many people died in the 1770 drought that it was not possible to count the totals.

The causes of hunger are often complicated by corruption, by black market dealing and by poor systems of distribution. Little seems to change through history. For example, in Russia, grain crop yields vary enormously from one year to the next because of variable weather. In 1972–73, the wheat crop alone was 10 million tonnes short. But at the same time, people in Russia also go hungry because the food distribution system is not effective. This was the situation in Russia in 1991 (see also page 42). In the autumn, the Russian president warned that revolts could break out if food shortages worsened and said, 'Naturally we could survive the winter more easily with Western help.' The seven richest industrial countries, known as the G7 group, agreed to help what was then the Soviet Union by giving it more time to repay its foreign debts.

On a world scale, the problems of hunger and famine are more severe today than at any time in the history of mankind. Every day, 10,000 people die of hunger and another 30,000 die of diseases associated with hunger.

Traditional harvesting in the Ukraine, Commonwealth of Independent States

Measuring the tragedy

One simple measure of hunger and starvation is the number of babies who die before reaching their first birthday. The number of babies who die out of every 1000 born alive is known as the Infant Mortality Rate (IMR).

In the map on page 9, a very simple version of IMR has been used. The countries shaded beige have an IMR of less than 50 per 1000. (This means that 49 or even fewer babies in each 1000 die before reaching their first birthday.) In these countries most of the people get enough to eat. These countries can either grow all the food that is needed for their people, or can grow some of it and buy the rest from other countries. All the developed countries belong to this group. A few of these countries produce more food than is needed. They sell surplus food to their neighbours, store it or give it away to countries with a high IMR.

The countries shaded brown on the map have an IMR of more than 50 per 1000. (That is, 50 or more babies in each 1000 die before reaching their first birthday.) In all these countries there is much hunger.

The countries where hunger is worst and most babies die used to be the African countries

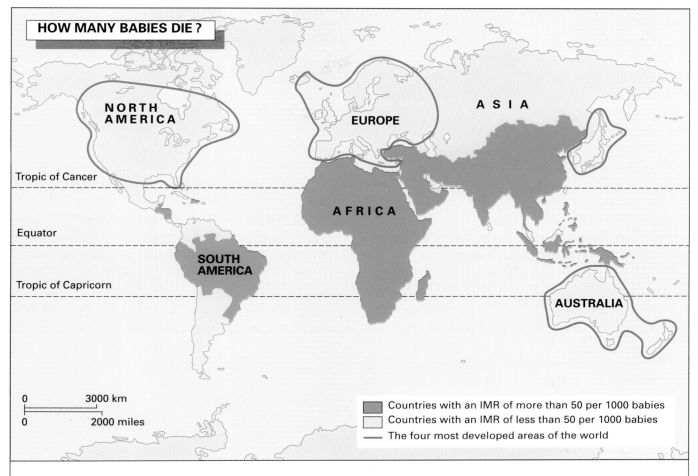

HOW MANY BABIES DIE ?

NORTH AMERICA

EUROPE

ASIA

AFRICA

SOUTH AMERICA

AUSTRALIA

Tropic of Cancer

Equator

Tropic of Capricorn

| 0 | 3000 km |
| 0 | 2000 miles |

■ Countries with an IMR of more than 50 per 1000 babies
□ Countries with an IMR of less than 50 per 1000 babies
— The four most developed areas of the world

The number of babies who die out of every 1000 born alive is known as the Infant Mortality Rate (IMR).
On this map, a simple version of IMR has been used.
At this scale it is not possible to show variations of IMR within countries (see page 10).

most affected by drought (see page 13). But the situation is changing. It is not that things are better in Africa; it is just that hunger has become even worse elsewhere. The highest numbers of infant deaths are now being recorded in parts of India and Pakistan, in Bangladesh, in Indonesia and in Mexico. In these countries, as in much of Africa, the IMR may be as high as 150 per 1000. But that is only an average figure. In the very worst disaster areas almost half the babies born die before they reach their first birthday.

Severely malnourished children attend a clinic in Macuba, Mozambique.

Cause and effect

There are many reasons why the IMR varies from one place to another and from one year to another. Here are some of the factors that can affect the IMR:

1 Natural disasters (droughts, earthquakes, volcanic eruptions and flooding).
2 The quality of the health services.
3 Very high birth rates. In some places, so many babies are being born that the country cannot possibly feed them.
4 The fact that some poor people are being pushed off their lands and are becoming refugees.
5 The mismanagement of resources by governments.
6 The amount of overseas aid being received.

In much of South Africa the wealthier and healthier white minority population has an IMR well below 50 per 1000. The much larger, and generally much poorer, black population has an IMR well above 50 per 1000.

In South America no country has an IMR as high as 200 per 1000. But inside some of these countries there are areas with an IMR as high as that. In Brazil the IMR among people who earn more than the average wage is never more than 50 per 1000. But among the poor of Brazil, living in city slums or driven off their lands by greedy ranchers, the IMR is often four times as high. Two hundred babies per 1000 die before their first birthday.

So there are variations inside countries, as well as between countries.

We can compare a developing country such as Brazil with the USA, which is about the same size but is a developed country. In the USA most of the hungry people are found in the slums of

A clinic for diarrhoeal diseases in Dhaka, Bangladesh. Many more clinics like this are needed to cope with the huge numbers of sick people in developing countries.

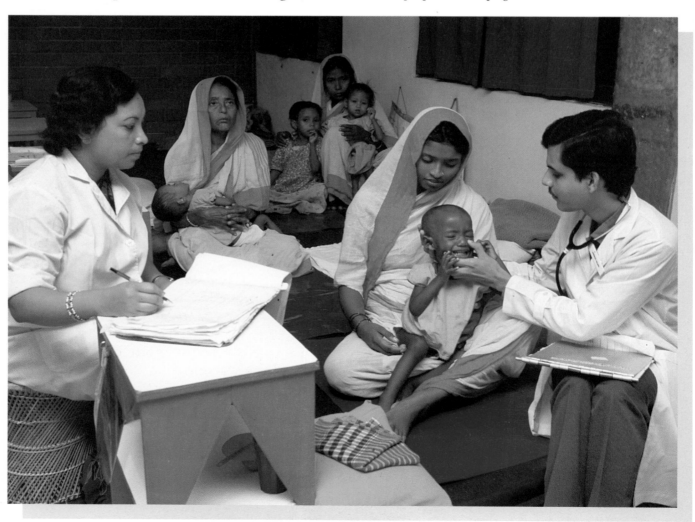

Slums in Rio de Janeiro, Brazil. Few people living here have either education or job opportunities.

big cities such as New York. There are about 20 million hungry in the USA. Unlike the situation in Brazil, almost all these people receive various kinds of cash benefits and social security support. Unfortunately, providing them with money does not always deal with their hunger. Some of these poor people spend the money on entertainment rather than good quality fresh food. Some spend most of their benefit payments on drugs and alcohol.

What we are learning from the poor of the developed lands such as the USA and Britain is that shortage of money is not the only problem. Other problems affect the hungry, including lack of education, lack of work and a lack of any sense of a decent future for themselves or their children. *The hungry are right.* There *is* no future for them without adequate housing, job opportunities and education.

In the poor countries of the developing world, money and food do help the starving to survive, but many of the hungry people now see little future for themselves outside the refugee camps. Small numbers of them are being resettled on the land but many of them are not.

Many of the hungry people were once living on their own lands, growing their own foods. They were not rich in money terms but their diet was healthy and adequate. But then they were pushed off their lands. Huge farms and ranches were created to produce foods such as peanuts and beef. This food was not produced for the local people but for export to the developed countries. The new farms only required a few workers, so most of the local peasant farmers lost both their land and any chance to earn money. Many of them are now found among the hungry of the city slums and refugee camps. None of the money earned by exporting food ever reaches them.

When we ask 'Who are the hungry?' the answer includes not just the victims of natural disasters such as earthquakes and droughts. The hungry include the people made hungry by the actions of others in their own country and elsewhere.

CHAPTER TWO

DISASTERS NATURAL AND UNNATURAL

Floods in Asia

In much of the world the farming systems that are used are in a state of delicate balance with Nature. The type of farming and the kinds of animals and crops are all closely related to the nature of the soils, the climate and the seasons. If the balance between people and land is maintained over many years then farming will be successful and the people can feed themselves. This is true for places as different as rice fields in China and wheat fields in France. Where the balance is kept there may even be a food surplus that can be traded for other goods, or sold for money. In some places this balance has existed undisturbed for hundreds of years.

A quite small change on one side of the balance can lead to disaster, at least for a short time. Fires, often started accidentally by lightning, can destroy field crops or tree crops. A period of exceptionally heavy rainfall may lead to flooding, soil erosion and the destruction of crops.

Survivors of floods in Bangladesh can only wait for water levels to go down.

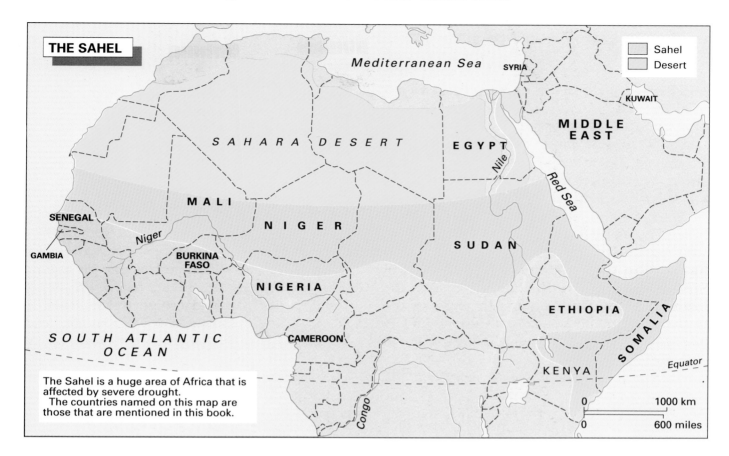

THE SAHEL

Mediterranean Sea

SYRIA

KUWAIT

MIDDLE EAST

SAHARA DESERT

EGYPT

Nile

Red Sea

MALI

SENEGAL

Niger

GAMBIA

BURKINA FASO

NIGER

SUDAN

NIGERIA

ETHIOPIA

SOUTH ATLANTIC OCEAN

CAMEROON

SOMALIA

KENYA

Equator

Congo

Sahel
Desert

0   1000 km

0   600 miles

The Sahel is a huge area of Africa that is affected by severe drought.
The countries named on this map are those that are mentioned in this book.

Bangladesh, perhaps more than any other country, is affected by sudden changes in the balance of Nature. This low-lying agricultural country on the great coastal delta of the River Ganges is too poor to spend money on any kind of major flood controls. Heavy monsoon season rains cause the River Ganges to rise and flood. If the rains are exceptionally heavy, or if a storm surge from the sea occurs at the same time, then the floods race uncontrolled across much of the country. The misery that results is reflected in the photograph on page 12 and in the eye-witness reports on page 7.

All the great rivers that enter Bangladesh have their sources hundreds of kilometres away in the Himalayas. They flood not just because of the rain that falls on Bangladesh itself but also because of the waters pouring out of the mountains.

There is some evidence that tree-felling in mountain countries such as Nepal is allowing rainwater to run off the mountains much faster and so increases flooding downstream in lowland India and Bangladesh. It is clear that only a huge *international* aid programme of river and flood control will help the people of Bangladesh.

Tragedy in the desert

Sudden climatic changes cause temporary hunger and suffering, but they are not usually a widespread cause of starvation. It is climatic changes that happen over a long period of time that are much more likely to cause severe problems of starvation.

The pattern of rainfall in the Sahel in Africa changed dramatically over several decades. A study of the annual rainfall between 1940 and 1985 shows that until 1970, groups of dry years were followed by wetter years, which helped to lessen the problems of drought and hunger. But since 1970, every year has had a rainfall total below the average annual rainfall. As the very limited rainfall has become less, and also become less reliable each year, so drought, hunger, famine and starvation have spread across huge areas of Africa. The famine here is more serious than any other famine in history.

As the years have passed the situation has become worse. For example, almost none of the trees that grow in the Sahel can survive a drought as long as seven years. Now the trees are dead they no longer protect the soil, and much of it has been blown away by the winds. To make things worse, there is now a shortage of every kind of timber. As a result, what little food the people have can no longer be cooked on wood fires. Undercooked food is not healthy food so diseases spread rapidly.

In 1991 an epidemic of meningitis affected the starving in southern Sudan in Africa. By the spring, 50,000 people had died of the disease, which is caused by infection and which affects the brain or spine.

This remote part of Africa has suffered years of drought and civil war. During the epidemic, medical supplies ran out and the only hospital closed down. Aid workers could not reach the region because of the fighting. The only way the local people could control the spread of the disease was to confine the sick in camps where they were left to die. One of the very few Europeans to reach the region described the situation:

Desert sands (below) are spreading into drought-damaged savannah grasslands in South Mali, Africa. In northern Kenya, a tree-planting project (below right) is helping to protect the soil from erosion.

These people are carrying earth to help build a road to their village in Ethiopia, as part of a 'food for work' scheme. In return, they receive wheat and cooking oil. In another part of the country, water in petrol tankers (inset) is delivered to herdsmen and their animals.

'There is no food of any sort to be found there. Everyone is hungry, people are eating leaves and even those with a few remaining cattle are slaughtering them to survive.
Every hut has at least one grave beside it; every family has been affected by meningitis, and hunger is making everyone weaker and weaker. There are months to go before any rains can begin or harvest be collected.'

It is now certain that several African countries in or near the Sahel will be affected by famine well into the twenty-first century. The balance between people and land has been terribly disturbed. The people in these drought-destroyed lands cannot put the balance right by themselves. They now need huge amounts of aid, and they need it every year.

Mismanaging the Earth

The spread of hunger and famine is not only the result of droughts or of any other natural disaster. It is often caused partly or almost entirely by how people disturb the balance between themselves and their environment.

Deforestation – the clearing of trees from the land – is one of many ways in which this balance can be upset. Once cleared, the land is used to grow crops or rear animals. In the USA virtually all the great forests had been cleared away by 1939. Now the tropical forests are being cleared away in many countries such as Brazil, Indonesia and Nigeria. Clearing continues even where little forest survives.

The worst effects of deforestation are felt by people living in areas of tropical forests that grow on poor soils. The local population has learned to clear only very small patches of forest at a time to grow their crops. After only two or three years they move to a new clearing, and the old one is allowed to become overgrown and return to forest. In this type of farming, sometimes called shifting agriculture, the land is allowed to rest after crop-growing. Wind and rain cause little damage to the soils in these small, sheltered clearings. When ranchers and grain farmers move into such areas they clear thousands of hectares of land at a time. The balance between people and land is im-

Cattle grazing on land cleared of forest in Amazonia, Brazil. The animals will soon strip the ground cover plants from the infertile soil.

mediately destroyed. The unprotected soils are soon completely exhausted and then destroyed by erosion. The ranchers move on, but the local people cannot move back and grow food because the land is no longer fertile. This has happened in many parts of the developing world that were once tropical forests, such as parts of Central America, Brazil and Indonesia.

Overgrazing is the result either of keeping too many animals on the land or of keeping animals in the same place for too long. The results are always the same. All the ground plants, such as grasses and herbs, are stripped off the land by the animals, leaving the soil bare and unprotected. Erosion quickly destroys these grazing lands, which once supported many people and their animals. Overgrazing can be caused by a variety of factors, including an increase in the birth rate of the people or their animals. A change in farming methods may also lead to overgrazing (see page 23).

Land is now also being lost to farming because it is being overcropped. If too many crops are grown, or if the same crop is grown every year, the land becomes exhausted. The land is never allowed to rest, to lie fallow. In several parts of the developing world where this is happening, the local farmers either cannot afford fertilisers or do not know how to use them. As the land becomes exhausted by overcropping so the crops become poorer.

In parts of Senegal in West Africa, a study of crop yields of peanuts showed that if the land was neither rested nor fertilised, crop yields fell by an average of 25 per cent per year. This kind of fall in crop production means that an area of land that fed 100 people in 1992 will only feed:

75 people in 1993,
56 people in 1994,
42 people in 1995,
32 people in 1996
and 24 people in 1997.

If we turn this last figure round then *in 1997 four times as much land will be needed to feed the same number of people as in 1992.*

The truth could be even worse than that. Some time before 1997 the land could be abandoned completely and the people moved to another place. The abandoned land may be so exhausted and neglected that it could be lost to farming for ever.

Water and salt

Irrigation farming is farming using water brought to the land artificially. The water may be sprayed on the land, poured or pumped through channels and ditches or allowed to flood fields next to a river.

The effect of irrigation is to increase crop yields by an enormous amount, in some cases by 500 per cent. This could mean that an area of land producing food for 100 people could then feed 500 people when it was irrigated. Fifty years ago many farming experts believed irrigation might solve the world's food shortages. Now they are not so sure. Things are going seriously wrong.

Some irrigation schemes feed water directly to plant roots but others simply flood the land. The salts in the irrigation water collect in the soil as the water is evaporated by the sun. Every year the amount of salts increases in the soil until it begins to destroy the roots of the crops.

Rice fields on terraced hillsides in the Philippines (main picture) are flooded by rainfall. Irrigation in a desert area of Arizona, USA, (inset) will lead to salinisation of the soil.

Land that once gave huge increases in crops because of irrigation now gives no crops at all.

This problem is found throughout the world. A travel writer in Iraq described the irrigated land there as being so full of salts that it seemed to be covered with fresh snow. Nothing was growing there.

This problem is called salinisation (making salty). The cure, or part cure, is called desalinisation, which means removing salts. The only satisfactory way to do this is to process the irrigation water in a desalinisation factory to remove all the salts. This process is enormously expensive. The only country in the table (below) where this might be possible is the USA. In all the poorer countries, once the land is ruined it may stay ruined for ever.

The amount of irrigated land partly or severely damaged by salinisation in six developed and developing countries, is as follows:

Egypt	80 per cent
Pakistan	70 per cent
Iraq	50 per cent
Peru	40 per cent
USA	30 per cent
India	20 per cent

Another problem with irrigation schemes is that for some of them the water has to be stored in the rainy season so that it can be used on the land in the dry season. One way of storing water is to build large dams across rivers.

The first disadvantage of dam-building is that a lot of good riverside farmlands are lost for ever under the lake behind the dam. The second is that a lot of the water is lost by evaporation from the surface of the lake. It never reaches the land downstream from the dam.

The third disadvantage is that when a river is dammed, all the silt (fine mud) it carries is trapped behind the dam. This damages the irrigation scheme in two ways. Firstly, the silt that used to spread out over the fields when they were flooded by the river no longer reaches them. This rich silt was a major source of plant foods for the land. Secondly, the trapped silt gradually fills up the lake behind the dam. When the lake is silted up it will no longer provide water for the farmlands downstream. It is now estimated that in the lower Nile valley, the Aswan Dam and Lake Nasser behind it will only be effective for water storage until about the year 2050. This is about half the length of time originally forecast.

These examples of mismanagement of the Earth, from deforestation, overgrazing and over-cropping to overwatering (irrigation), show how the balance between people and land can be destroyed. In many cases this destruction is completed in as few as three or four years. The local people themselves are often aware of what is going wrong, that new developments show no respect for the earth. In Niger in West Africa, local people in some country areas have asked the government to close down new wells and not to dig any others. They have recognised that the new wells are bringing too many animals and too many people on to their fragile land.

But all too often the local people are ignored by government. Dams for water and for electric power are often built to serve the cities rather than the country. Great irrigation schemes, cattle ranches and forest clearances are decided upon for reasons of greed and political power. The people who actually live on the land are not often consulted.

Even if the wishes of local people are considered, there are two huge pressures operating in the world that prevent those wishes being put into action. These pressures are discussed in the next chapter.

Local farmers in Third World countries can be efficient and productive when unaffected by disasters, or interference from First World countries. These traditional stacks of sorghum (right) are in Cameroon, West Africa.

The Aswan Dam, Egypt

CHAPTER THREE

TOO MANY PEOPLE

Two vital factors are always acting against the hungry people of the world.

1 World population is increasing far faster than food supplies.
2 All the developed countries are increasing their demands for food.

The expected growth of world population is shown on the map on this page. The map shows that all the countries in which population will increase by more than 100 per cent in the next 30 years are *all* in the developing world. The countries with the largest increases are likely to be the very poorest countries: the Third World.

This means that most of the biggest increases in population will take place in the countries least able to cope with population increase. In these countries, for example most African countries, millions of people are starving *now*. For these people, the outlook would still be bleak even if the population figures remained stable.

Every day of the year about 250,000 babies are born into our already overcrowded world. Ninety per cent of these babies, that is 225,000 per day, are born in the developing world. The situation in the developed world is rather different. Here the expected increases in population will be less than 100 per cent. In several

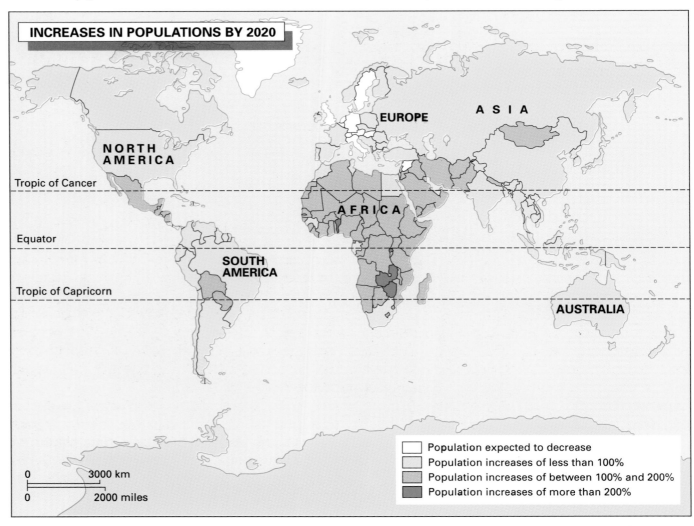

INCREASES IN POPULATIONS BY 2020

ASIA

EUROPE

NORTH AMERICA

Tropic of Cancer

AFRICA

Equator

SOUTH AMERICA

Tropic of Capricorn

AUSTRALIA

0   3000 km

0   2000 miles

☐ Population expected to decrease
☐ Population increases of less than 100%
☐ Population increases of between 100% and 200%
☐ Population increases of more than 200%

10,000 million mouths to feed

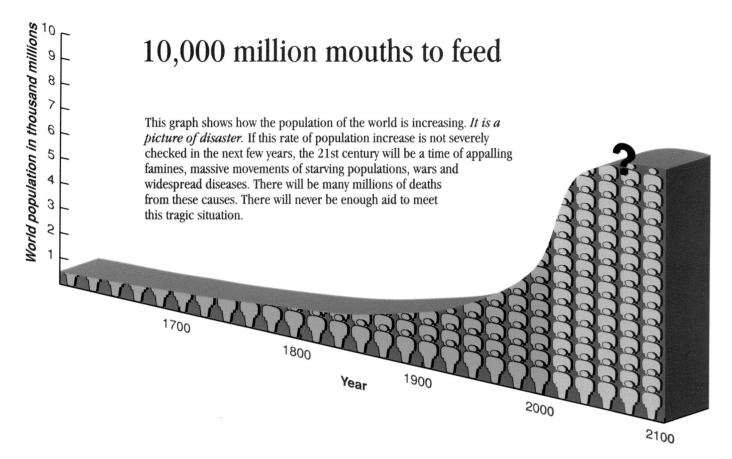

This graph shows how the population of the world is increasing. *It is a picture of disaster.* If this rate of population increase is not severely checked in the next few years, the 21st century will be a time of appalling famines, massive movements of starving populations, wars and widespread diseases. There will be many millions of deaths from these causes. There will never be enough aid to meet this tragic situation.

World population in thousand millions

Year

European countries, including Britain, there will even be a decline in the size of the population by the year 2020. The only countries outside Europe that are expected to show a population decrease early in the next century are Greenland and Syria.

However, other parts of the developed world will continue to show quite large population increases, although they will be less than 100 per cent. The combined population of the USA and Canada is expected to increase by about 25 per cent. This will give another 55 million mouths to feed. In total the developed lands will see their populations increase by about 250 million people by the year 2020. This is more than the present population of the USA.

The world map of expected population increases gives one picture of the situation. It is a gloomy picture. Real hope for the hungry would be shown only if all the countries of the world could be shown in white like a few of the European countries (see page 20).

The map shows percentage increase of population in relation to country. If we look at the increase of population in relation to time, the picture is even more frightening. That is the picture shown in the graph on this page.

The population explosion

The graph shows that world population increase has got faster and faster since 1700 AD. This huge increase in population is called the population explosion. In the last 15 years the world population has increased from 4000 million to 5000 million. But all the signs suggest that even this increase is being exceeded now. By the year 2100 the world population may be double what it was in 1991. Not only does this represent an enormous increase in the number of mouths to feed, it also means huge increases in the number of young people. One estimate is that half the population of Africa will be under the age of 14 by the year 2025. Most of them will be living in rural or urban poverty, most will be hungry and most will have no job prospects.

In every country of the world the reasons for the population explosion are being argued. People are puzzled that in a time when we know more about birth control than ever before the population explosion is still taking place.

There are two explanations for the population explosion that many people now accept.

Firstly, improvements in medical and health care allow many people to live much longer. This has increased population as more people live into old age. But even more important is the fact that population has increased simply because more people have lived long enough to become parents.

The second explanation is rather more complicated. The population explosion is worst in the Third World countries (see pages 9 and 20), but it was not always like that. In the past, many family and tribal groups practised their own methods of contraception and restricted the size of their families. They kept a healthy balance between their numbers and their land resources. Old people were looked after by their family and tribe.

One factor that destroyed this balance was development. Farmlands began to be used to produce crops for export to the developed world. People were pushed off their lands and so had no means of support. Because this happened so quickly, and in relatively poor countries, such things as state aid and help for the aged were never set up.

The only way to be cared for when old was by having many children. Each child was too poor to look after his parents by himself, especially if he had married and got a family of his own. But if there were eight or nine brothers and sisters (better still, 13 or 14) they might just manage to support each other, their parents and grandparents. As families have become poorer, the size of families has got bigger.

In a desperate attempt to survive, many people, having lost their land, are moving to the towns to find work. They now live in great shanty towns, earning a few pence a day. Not only is population exploding, it is becoming urban. This drift to the towns has been described as one of the greatest tragedies in the history of mankind. Countries affected by these changes include Sudan, Mali, Indonesia, the Philippines, parts of India, Brazil and Bolivia.

Tawawa Refugee Settlement in East Sudan. Most of the refugees here have crossed the border from Ethiopia.

This Bombay slum has grown partly as a result of the drift to the towns in India.

These two explanations for the population explosion are not the only ones. Other causes may also operate. For example, in some countries there are religious objections to the use of any kind of contraception. Poverty and ignorance also limit the use of contraception and so contribute to the population explosion.

The demand for food

A baby born in Europe or America will, on average, take about 40 times as much of the world's resources such as food and fuel as a baby born in Bangladesh or another Third World country. In other words, 40 Bangladeshi babies have to survive on what is available for just one European or American baby. It is not surprising that several of them will die before their first birthday, and the survivors go hungry for the rest of their short lives. At least half of the 40 Bangladeshi babies will have died by the

A shopping mall in Kyoto, Japan (below) contrasts with the poverty of a Bombay slum (see photograph on page 22).

time the European or American baby has grown to the age of 35.

As the baby born in the developed world begins to grow it uses more energy, wears more clothes, and eats far more food than a Third World baby. If in adult life the developed world baby becomes a parent, he or she will expect his or her children to have an even better start in life.

People in the developed world are only just beginning to realise how much of the world's food they demand. They are only just beginning to understand that some of that food is taken away from the hungry peoples of the world.

Cash crops: peanuts

In many of the poorest countries the local people were once able to feed themselves, and knew how to manage their lands to prevent the effects of overcropping or overgrazing. But now their lands are often used to produce crops to sell to the developed countries instead of growing the food they need for themselves. These crops for sale are called cash crops. For example, peanuts have been grown in some parts of the Sahel in Africa, especially in Niger (see the map on page 13). Local farmers were encouraged and supported by European businessmen to grow peanuts for export to Europe.

Before this, local farmers and cattle rearers had always rested the land for a few years. They let it lie fallow. Then the cattle were grazed on the fallow land, adding manure to the soil. The lands then gave good crops for the next two or three years. This rotation of land use kept the system working. Then, as peanut farming spread, more and more fallow land was ploughed up. The fallow was no longer rested, nor used as grazing. The cattle rearers were driven out to the desert edge.

At the same time the farmers were getting into debt buying new seed, new equipment and fertilisers that did not really restore the exhausted soil. Peanut plants very quickly exhaust the soil. The land needs about six years to recover from three years of peanut farming. Then between 1967 and 1969 the price farmers were paid for peanuts fell by more than 25 per cent.

The desperate farmers now had to grow peanuts on another 25 per cent of their land just to pay the interest on the debts they already had. In Niger the area under peanuts grew by 400 per cent between 1954 and 1968. 1968 was the year the droughts began (see page 13).

No one can say how many of the thousands who died of starvation might have lived if traditional farming methods had still been in use. What is certain is that by the time the droughts came, large areas of cropland and semi-desert were so damaged there was almost no plant cover left. Neither the farmers nor the cattle herdsmen could survive the droughts. What makes this tragedy worse is that, in much of Europe, we do not even regard peanuts as a meal. They are a party snack or something to eat at the cinema.

When we read of these tragedies and see pictures of starving people on television most of us want to do two things. We want to help, and we want to blame somebody. But before we blame anybody at all we need to consider other examples of land 'development'. Unfortunately there are hundreds of such examples.

A peanut farmer in Madagascar. Much of his crop will be exported.

The case of the American hamburger

Most hamburgers are really beefburgers. The meat in them comes from cattle. Since 1965 the number of beef cattle in Central American countries such as Costa Rica has increased by 70 per cent. It has been estimated that almost 90 per cent of the beef produced has been exported to the USA. Much of it was used in hamburgers. This cheaper, leaner beef held down the price of burgers in the USA by only about five cents per pound. But the real cost of this saving was enormous.

To produce just one hamburger requires the destruction and clearance of nearly six square metres of tropical forest in Central America. The forest is cleared *for ever*; within three or four years the land is exhausted by the grazing cattle and begins to be eroded by the heavy rains. The same has happened to the lands of the local people who were forced to move to make way for the cattle ranchers. Almost none of the beef that is produced on these lands feeds the local people. They cannot afford it. A statistic that is often quoted is that by 1985 the average Costa Rican was eating less beef than the average American domestic cat.

The case of the cotton shirt

In the last 20 years there has been a big increase in the amount of cotton grown in the Sudan. Almost all of it is a cash crop for export to Europe. The Sudanese government moved thousands of small farmers off their lands so that cotton fields could be laid out. Almost none of the profits reached the people who were made homeless by this development.

Between 1980 and 1990 the rise in cotton production was matched by the fall in sorghum production – the main food crop. Stocks of sorghum stored in the towns were not distributed to the starving in the countryside but were sold to the townspeople. Prices rose to 25 times the original price. This greed and selfishness has been a contributing factor to the start of the civil war. (See page 31.)

Cotton waiting to be exported from Mali

A woman picking cotton in Swaziland, Africa

Other cases tell similar stories. In Indonesia, in southeast Asia, the government has been organising a programme of land reforms that has made 12 million people homeless in the last 10 years. The land reforms are designed to benefit a few rich landowners. Protesters are labelled troublemakers or communists and thrown into jail. There is no trial. During this programme of land reform the IMR in Indonesia has risen to become one of the highest in the world.

In Ethiopia, people starve and die of thirst while the country exports water melons. While people are short of protein in their diet in Gambia, that country, like Niger, exports peanuts, which are rich in protein.

It is clear that hunger and famine are almost never the result of one single cause. There is almost never just one event or one country to blame. In fact, blaming is a waste of energy. The truth is that in one way or another we are all to blame to some extent. What matters is not blaming but asking what needs to be changed in order to save the lives of 40,000 people a day. The vital question is how can we help? Much of the rest of this book is about this question.

CHAPTER FOUR

AID AND RESCUE

The countries of the world that offer aid to others are called donor countries. The countries receiving aid are called recipient countries. In addition to giving international aid, developed countries also have schemes for aiding and rescuing the hungry and homeless who live inside their own boundaries. This kind of internal aid often passes almost unnoticed, and is not always supported by the public as wholeheartedly as international aid usually is. We may find it easier to be sympathetic towards the victims of drought and civil war in Africa than towards the victims of our own society who live in the slums of major cities.

Donor countries offer aid to the recipient countries in many ways. The four main types of aid are food, money, skills and military aid.

All the developed countries are donor countries, giving aid. All the Third World countries are recipient countries, receiving aid. They include African countries in the Sahel, countries of Central America, Cambodia and Bangladesh. Some countries that are now succeeding in developing (see page 7) are both donors and recipients, giving and receiving aid. They include Brazil, India and Egypt. Kuwait is an example of a country that gives some kinds of aid, such as foods and technical skills, and receives other kinds of aid, such as military aid.

Food aid represents only about 10 per cent of the value of all aid offered, but it is especially

Stacks of rice at Dakar Docks in Senegal, Africa waiting to be sent inland to drought-stricken areas

important for two reasons. First, it is the kind of aid most of us are concerned about. It seems only sensible to send food to the starving. Second, what the donor and recipient countries do with food aid reveals what is really going on with most kinds of aid.

People living in the donor countries often believe that sending food to the hungry and starving is the best thing to do. It seems the simplest and most direct way to help those most in need. Sadly, this is often untrue. In fact, there is even some evidence that sending food to other countries sometimes causes harm.

Donor countries send food aid in three main ways:
1 as emergency aid, a once-only rescue aid for the starving.
2 as project aid, food given as 'pay' for work on projects.
3 as programme aid, regular donations of food which can either be distributed to the hungry or sold to raise money for projects.

Road communications are so poor in Third World countries that food loads have to be broken down into individual sacks in order to get them to the hungry people in the countryside (above and below).

Emergency food aid

This aid is usually a single donation of food made to the disaster area of an earthquake, flood or famine. When famine is caused by long periods of drought, then the food aid may become regular aid through the drought years. This happened in parts of the Sahel where there has been almost continuous drought since 1968 (see page 13).

The biggest problem with emergency food aid is that it usually arrives too late. By 1980 the effect of the drought years in the Sahel led the United Nations Food and Agricultural Organisation to warn the world that hunger was turning to famine. Almost nothing was done. Action did not really begin until the end of 1984, after television reports about the starving people caused an outcry. It was public protest, rather than government planning, that got food aid moving.

Despite this, it took over a year – 400 days – before any food promised by the EC actually reached Africa. By then, millions had died and 35 million people were starving in 20 countries.

By the time the food did arrive, people had moved to refugee camps. If food had reached them while they were still in their villages they might have been able to repair some of the damage. Instead, the camps became their permanent homes, and the land was abandoned.

Another problem with emergency food aid is that it often arrives from several countries at the same time. The recipient countries cannot cope with all the food. They cannot store it, transport it or issue it fast enough. Enormous quantities are wasted, while out in the countryside people are dying. It is estimated that only about three quarters of the food received in Ethiopia was ever distributed to hungry people. In the Sudan, only about 65 per cent reached the hungry.

Yet another complication was that food that the donor countries wanted to get rid of was not always suitable for the people in the recipient countries. This led to health problems, to changes in diet and, in some cases, even to the collapse of local farming, because people no longer wanted to eat locally-grown foods.

In some recipient countries not so seriously affected by drought, food aid started to arrive just as the local harvests improved. Local crops

Food is distributed to the hungry in the drought-stricken region of Korem, Ethiopia.

rotted in the fields because the warehouses were full of food from the EC and the USA. Local farmers were ruined; they abandoned their lands and became hungry refugees in the towns. In some countries the local people demonstrated *against* the arrival of food aid. In countries as far apart as Kenya and Haiti, food aid did harm as well as helping.

Project aid

Project aid schemes offer local people food in return for working on local projects designed to improve their homeland. These projects are often quite beyond the resources of the local people working alone. For example, schemes such as marsh drainage, desert reclamation by planting drought-resistant plants and tree planting to reduce soil erosion cannot be carried out

Local farmers are lining an irrigation canal in Qinghai Province, China, with help from the United Nations World Food Programme.

Ethiopian refugees who have fled to a camp in the Sudan are harvesting aubergines as part of a German aid project.

by local farmers working alone. They lack the money for equipment, they may lack technical skills, and may know nothing about results from agricultural research. But if some or all of these things are offered by their government or by a relief agency from a donor country, local farmers can offer their labour.

The result is a double benefit. During a year of food shortages they receive food for their families. The work they do helps to improve their homeland for the years when they can farm again. One of several successful schemes was the work in hill country in Ethiopia to plant trees and build hill terraces to control soil erosion and conserve water. Each worker was paid with enough food for a family of six. Over half the workers said the scheme had saved their families from starvation during the worst famine years.

This kind of aid is obviously very valuable. It prevents starvation and it involves the local people in working for their own *local* benefit by improving their homeland. It can also help to develop links between the donors and the recipients.

But just as with emergency food aid, things can go wrong. The most serious problem is that if too many healthy and fit local people are drawn into the scheme their own farms may be neglected. They may also consider the scheme an easier way of getting food for their families than struggling to grow it themselves. The workers may become too dependent on the food-for-work scheme. This kind of aid has to be carefully planned to encourage workers to keep their own drought-damaged farms in operation, even if crops are very poor for some years.

Other problems arise when the government of the recipient country makes political decisions about which schemes shall be developed first. For example, if food is given for improving roads between cities this may do almost nothing to help farmers in the most rural areas. In Third World countries damaged by civil war, the governments may only be interested in schemes that help them fight the rebels. The needs of the hungry are placed second to feeding the troops and improving roads for moving armies about

Building a well near Djibouti, in East Africa. This is part of a long-term European aid project.

Emergency food aid for the hungry in a refugee camp in Mexico

the country. It may be very difficult for aid workers from donor countries to do anything at all about this. They are in the recipient country as visitors and can easily be thrown out.

Programme food aid

The basic idea behind programme food aid is that the donor country shall give regular donations of food aid to the government of the recipient country. This food aid can either be stored as reserves for the people or it can be sold. If it is sold the money will then be spent on agreed development projects. Seventy per cent of all food aid takes this form. Unfortunately, this major kind of food aid almost never reaches the poor and hungry in the recipient countries.

There are many reasons for this. One is that the political decision of recipient governments is to look after the people most likely to support them. Much of the food aid is sold to people in the towns who can afford to buy it and who are not hungry in the first place, including government employees, civil servants, businessmen and the armed forces. The hungry people out in the countryside rarely see any of this food. It is not surprising that in several countries torn

apart by civil war the first rebellions began in the countryside and led to attacks on the towns.

A second reason for food aid not reaching the hungry is that it is often extremely difficult to get food into the countryside. The ports, the railways and the better roads all serve the main cities. Many rural areas are connected only by dirt tracks. For food loads to reach rural areas they have to be broken down into individual sacks and boxes to be carried by camels and donkeys. Much of this food is lost or damaged on the journey. (See page 27.)

The failure of much programme aid is also the responsibility of the donor countries. Firstly, most of the donor countries pay their own farmers to produce huge food surpluses. The food is expensive to produce and expensive to store. This may be a political decision, a way of overpaying farmers to obtain their votes. The surplus food is then sent to the recipient countries, whether or not it is suitable food. It has become part of a deal to support developing countries important to the rich nations.

Two outstanding example of this are the aid (and interference) inflicted on countries close to the Suez and Panama Canals. Just as some of these countries have been attacked by the USA and European countries at different times, so they have been bribed with enormous amounts of food aid. For example, of all the cereals shipped to African countries in 1985–86, over half went to just one country: Egypt. To make matters worse, the people of Egypt do not need as much food aid as most other African countries. But Egypt's control of the Suez Canal, and its more pro-western attitudes than those of some other countries, ensure that huge quantities of food are sent there. In Egypt, bread has become as cheap as chicken feed.

Meanwhile, in the countries where many are starving, the food there is just too expensive for the poor to buy it. Many people who die of starvation do so not because there is no food but because they cannot afford it.

Food aid of various kinds does help the hungry and starving, but far less of it reaches the hungry than is realised by the people in the donor countries. If the donor countries intend to go on helping the hungry of the world they need to find better ways of doing so. Aid and rescue in the 1990s needs to be far better organised than it was in the 1980s.

The Suez Canal, Egypt, provides a direct link between the Mediterranean Sea and the Indian Ocean.

Winnowing the grain in Bolivia. In many small communities in the developing world, traditional methods need to be improved rather than completely replaced.

The diagram (right) compares two methods of giving aid to developing countries.

Reorganising aid

The pattern in the past

The developed world demands cash crops such as, cotton, peanuts and coffee.

Plant cover destroyed to grow cash crops

soil erosion, herds overgraze

local food production reduced

No response from the developed world.

→ hunger

Rains fail → hunger → starvation

When the developed countries send aid, it may arrive too late for the starving people.

Land abandoned → refugee camps

The pattern in the future

The developed world demands far fewer cash crops than in the past.

Far less plant cover is destroyed.

Crops fail if rains fail → hunger

Donor countries respond quickly. Emergency food aid is sent

→ immediate emergency food aid

Other kinds of aid are given to help provide a sustainable way of life.

Other aid → tree planting, restocking, etc.

Conditions stabilise → people stay →

land restored → conditions improve.

CHAPTER FIVE

MAKING REPAIRS

Looking to the future

A huge proportion of the aid offered to the hungry does nothing whatever to prevent them becoming hungry again in the near future. Sometimes the aid is so misdirected it may even do more harm than good. We offer the hungry and homeless in our cities better blankets so they will be more comfortable sleeping in shop doorways. We send completely unsuitable foods from Europe to Africa simply because we want to get them out of our warehouses. Some of these foods actually make hungry Africans ill. These kinds of help do nothing to repair the damage in any way that holds out the hope of a better future. The only aid that really helps to repair the damage is aid that gives the hungry a future as well as a meal today. Emergency aid is vital but it must be linked to long-term improvements in the life situations of the hungry.

Here is an example of this kind of aid. In northern Kenya, the Samburu and Turkana peoples raise animals in an area of semi-arid grasslands. Droughts are not uncommon but the people have developed ways of rearing their animals that take this into account. They move their herds according to the seasons from one area of grazing to another, which helps to prevent overgrazing the poor lands they live on.

In 1984 there was a drought. Unfortunately, there was an epidemic of livestock diseases at the same time. In some herds, as many as 80 per cent of the goats, cattle and sheep died. The people lost not only their own source of food, but also the skins and hides they traded for other kinds of food.

Emergency food supplies were distributed by

Samburu tribesmen with their herds

Ethiopian refugees in Tawawa Camp (see page 22) learning new skills in metalworking

Oxfam, but it was linked with plans to repair the damage. The local people discussed their needs in detail and an animal-restocking programme was launched. Families were given or loaned small starter flocks of sheep and herds of goats. They were also given a few donkeys and camels as pack animals. With these new animals the refugees were able to leave the camps and move out into the grasslands again. The restocking programme was followed up with improvements in marketing the skins and hides, and with the provision of training in the use of drugs for animal health. The emergency was dealt with and *at the same time* important steps were taken to improve the future prospects of the local people.

One of the ways in which help is most needed is in the area of education in its widest meaning. For example, people living in areas affected by the advance of the desert and the destruction of grasslands may be accustomed to periods of hunger and food shortages. They might be quite ignorant of the signs that hunger is becoming starvation. In Ethiopia in the 1980s Save the Children Fund workers trained local people in nutrition and diet so that they could recognise the onset of famine. As a result, earlier warning of approaching disaster was possible. When emergency food aid did eventually arrive it could be directed to the areas where it was most needed. Local people can now keep a permanent check on the seriousness of hunger in their home areas.

A plan to follow

These two example of making repairs, one in Kenya and one in Ethiopia, illustrate some vital points about what makes aid effective.

1 **Effective aid comes more often from agencies at work than from government aid.** Although aid from governments far exceeds agency aid in amounts, it is often far less effective. There are many reasons for this:
   - relief agencies have less money to spend so spend it carefully, which means in consultation with the local people.
   - because offering aid is their first and main aim they are very good at doing that, and have experienced fieldworkers to call on.
   - much of the administration of aid is carried out in the recipient country, and not in the donor country.
   - because much of agency finance is raised directly from the general public, the agencies feel directly accountable to the public.
   (So effective are some relief agencies that government funds are now being given directly to them instead of being used only by government organisations.)

2 **Effective aid is often a package of measures.** It is not only a matter of food supplies, it also involves health issues, education, training and skills development for the local

people. For example, provision of food aid may be linked with supplies of seed or animals for the years following the famine. Farming and veterinary techniques may be improved.

3 **Effective aid is concerned with making repairs and improvements that are sustainable.** This means the help offered leads to long-term improvements which the local people can maintain over many years. A well-known example of this kind of sustainable and long-lasting improvement has been the development of 'stone lines' in Burkina Faso. Lines of local stones laid out parallel to the slope of the ground reduce soil erosion and retain rainwater in the soil. Crop yields have risen by as much as 50 per cent. The simple skills needed to do this can be learned in a morning, and carried out entirely by local people.

4 **Effective aid is organised in partnership with the local people.** An outstanding example is the development of the Green Belt Movement in Kenya. Led by a remarkable woman, Professor Wangari Maathai, the people of Kenya have planted out more than 10 million native trees. Most of this work has been done by women. It is the women who grow more than three quarters of Kenya's food and collect three quarters of the firewood. The combination of replanting the eroded lands and protecting the farmlands at the same time is vital to the long-term future of the country. The development of new woodlands and tree nurseries has received some help from overseas aid agencies but it has been almost entirely managed and carried out by the people themselves. They work at it because they can see how it benefits them.

As these successful schemes multiply, the basic message is beginning to be understood in both the donor and recipient countries. Repairing the damage is only effective if the aid is appropriate to the local area and does not damage the local environment. Apart from emergency aid to meet a particular famine situation, all aid needs to lead to sustainable improvements which involve the local people in feeding themselves more effectively on their own lands.

Farming the desert

An impressive example of local development in Kenya is the Baobab Farm near Mombasa. The site was once a desert landscape in an abandoned coral limestone quarry. The development has been based on agroforestry, a system of farming in which trees and crops are grown together and animals are raised that can feed on some of the plants being grown.

One type of tree, the casuarina, has grown particularly well on the bare, rock-hard earth. It produces its own nitrate fertiliser from chemicals in the air and soil, while the roots break up the rocks and the falling leaves add compost to the ground. These trees grow very fast and produce wood for fuel within five years. Later their straight trunks are used for building.

The animals are chosen so they can be reared together without destroying the new vegetation. Sheep outnumber goats ten to one, because they are less destructive. Cattle graze alongside local species of deer — the deer eat different grasses from those eaten by cattle and also produce good quality meat.

The theme of inter-relatedness also affects the way water is used on the farm. Fast-growing tilapia fish are bred in tanks to provide more protein in the African diet. Dirty water from the fish tanks is pumped on to rice fields. The rice crop feeds on the fish waste in the water, which is then purified and recycled elsewhere.

Another scheme being tested on the farm is the rearing of baby crocodiles, both for their valuable skins and for their meat. The crocodiles are fed with offal from the animals and the fish. Nothing is wasted.

The farm has been running for 30 years and attracts many visitors. Several other abandoned local quarries have now been involved in the scheme. An education and training programme is a vital part of the work. The message to Kenyan farmers is clear: 'If this can be done on one of the worst sites on Earth, what might you do with your farms and ponds?'

The coral limestone quarry before being reclaimed for farming

The reclaimed quarry a few years later, with casuarina trees being felled

Local species of deer, including eland and oryx, are being moved in to replace imported cattle.

The tilapia fish farm

Rice fields being prepared in the quarry

CHAPTER SIX

ONE WORLD

Lessons learned

The hungry and starving enter our living rooms on television and through the newspapers. The people of the developed world can no longer plead ignorance about what is happening in the Third World. Nor can they pretend it is nothing to do with them. We all live in one world, and this world is all we have. The media have done us a great service by bringing us news of the hungry in our world and by showing us that perhaps we are all partly responsible for much of their hunger. We may not be comfortable with this news but we cannot deny it.

We know that western-style development schemes fail in most countries that are not western. (Japan is in some ways the notable exception.) Western schemes have made the people poorer, devastated their environments and left their countries crippled with debts.

We know that the hungry are also the poor. In many countries they would not be so hungry if food prices were not kept so high.

We also know that the most successful aid from donor countries is aid that recognises the needs of the recipient. It is aid that allows the recipients to make sustainable improvements in their environment.

A better way to help?

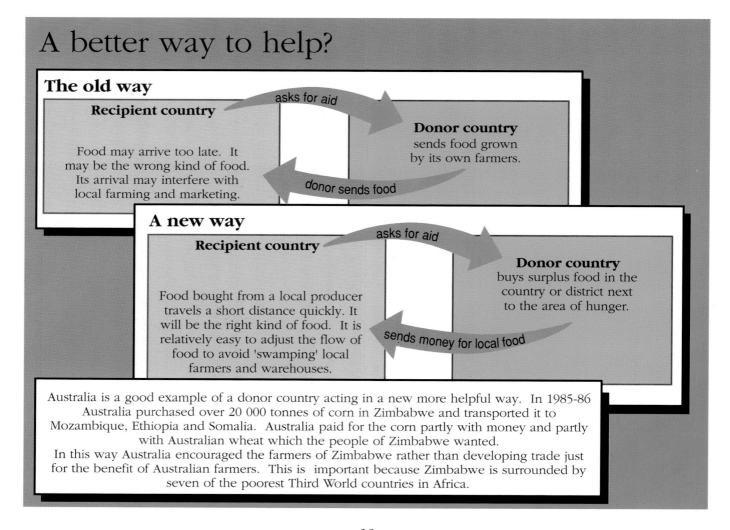

The old way

Recipient country

asks for aid

Food may arrive too late. It may be the wrong kind of food. Its arrival may interfere with local farming and marketing.

donor sends food

Donor country
sends food grown by its own farmers.

A new way

Recipient country

asks for aid

Food bought from a local producer travels a short distance quickly. It will be the right kind of food. It is relatively easy to adjust the flow of food to avoid 'swamping' local farmers and warehouses.

sends money for local food

Donor country
buys surplus food in the country or district next to the area of hunger.

Australia is a good example of a donor country acting in a new more helpful way. In 1985-86 Australia purchased over 20 000 tonnes of corn in Zimbabwe and transported it to Mozambique, Ethiopia and Somalia. Australia paid for the corn partly with money and partly with Australian wheat which the people of Zimbabwe wanted.
In this way Australia encouraged the farmers of Zimbabwe rather than developing trade just for the benefit of Australian farmers. This is important because Zimbabwe is surrounded by seven of the poorest Third World countries in Africa.

Drought refugees in a make-shift shelter in Mali

Changing lifestyles

Despite our growing understanding of the causes of hunger and the plight of the hungry, the situation is getting worse. Public opinion in the developed lands is increasingly aroused to protest and to help. But the reality of one world and one family of man living in it is still not accepted by many people when it threatens their own standard of living. For example, some people who give money to charities helping with food aid may not be so ready to change their own eating habits. Yet the evidence suggests that a diet based largely on meat is incredibly wasteful of the world's resources. Animals reared for meat eat over 40 per cent of

all the grains grown in the world. If those grains were fed directly to people they would feed ten times as many as are fed by the meat.

The developed countries still want to believe that their way of doing things is sustainable. But is it? For example, American and European farmers produce vast quantities of good quality foods, but their methods are very inefficient. Huge quantities of energy and other resources are used up in machinery, fuels, services, labour and distribution costs. A Chinese farmer is about 500 times more efficient than a European farmer in the use of resources (see page 40).

The developed countries maintain their lifestyles by importing huge quantities of foods from developing countries. Almost twice as much

Rice being transplanted into paddy fields
Rice growing in paddy fields in Canton, China (right)

Threshing rice to separate the grain from the plant

Harvested rice drying in the sun

In some parts of the world, rice is the staple food. Rice cultivation in much of southern China is an example of very efficient farming by the local people. High yields are produced in return for quite low inputs of energy resources. In many cases, local communities can produce enough rice not only for themselves but also for export to other areas.

The money business

Wheat harvest in Montana, USA. Wheat surpluses are a common feature of agricultural production in the developed world but require very high inputs of energy resources.

food leaves the developing countries as enters them, even allowing for all the food aid. To underline this imbalance, it is worth pointing out that the developing countries are obliged to sell the best of their products, and the rich nations often send them the products they do not need.

The western way of life is being undermined not by an enemy outside but by enemies within. The enemies who are almost literally eating up western societies are the affluent people who are always demanding more: more for themselves, and even more for their children. *But the message from our planet is that there is no more.* The only thing we are certain to have more of is mouths to feed.

The imbalance between the rich and the poor is far greater than is generally believed. For example, even if the size of the population of the USA remained exactly the same for the next 50 years, the growing demands of that population would increase and be almost insupportable by the rest of the world.

Another major area of difficulty is that the developed world is tied up in a money economy. Profit is measured in money, not in how many people have enough to eat.

The values of this money economy have been imposed on the developing countries, which have been burdened with money debts for technical help, for construction materials and so on. The poor countries have been expected to repay debts with interest rates that they could never hope to meet. When developing countries do enter world trade they find that prices are determined by the rich countries. The people who produce the tea, coffee, peanuts, cotton and tropical fruits have little say in what they are paid. Helping the hungry is still being treated as a financial business. In the five years from 1984 to 1989 there was a move of resources from poor countries to the rich of almost 140 billion dollars.

The peoples of the developed world still want to believe that their way of doing things is the best and only way. For example, the World Bank is supporting reforestry schemes in many countries. This recognises the intimate connection between trees and protection of croplands, between firewood and safe diet based on properly cooked food. But the trees planted have often been those suited to the needs of the international paper industry and not to the needs of the local people. Fast-growing trees that show a quick return on investment are often trees that most deplete the soil. As a result the land is rapidly impoverished. By the time those trees are felled the land has been robbed of its fertility.

The conditions imposed by wealthy countries offering loans are often very damaging to the poorer countries. A country borrowing money may be told:
– to reduce expenditure on health programmes and food subsidies,
– to reduce workers' wages,
– to grow crops for export to earn money to repay the debt, instead of growing food for the local people.
Such conditions hit hardest at the poor and hungry sections of the local community.

The heart of the matter

It is easy enough to criticise the rich countries and overlook their good intentions, but perhaps they should heed the words of the Swiss psychologist Carl Jung: 'Never know first; never know best'. It is also easy to overlook the extent to which the rich and poor countries are suffering from the same problems. A survey by the EC countries revealed that of all the food sent to Bangladesh, only one third ever reaches the poor and hungry. The rest has been diverted and sold at cut prices to the well-fed who can afford to buy it. Government employees were favoured by rationing schemes devised by the government. Greed is found in rich and poor countries alike.

In some African countries food does not reach the hungry because of distribution problems. But similar problems are now being experienced in Russia and the former Soviet republics. The food is not reaching the people because the government distribution system is breaking down and the black market is taking over. Black market prices for food stolen or 'lost' in the system are too high for the hungry and poor to pay. (See also page 8.)

Although enormous quantities of food (such as tomatoes, main picture) are grown in the Russian States, the distribution of food to towns and cities is very poorly organised. The appearance of a food delivery truck is enough to cause a queue to form (inset).

However, we are slowly discovering how to help the hungry of the world by processes of trial and error that have cost millions of lives. We see the sense of giving help that is of long-term value. We see the sense of being ready to help in emergencies. If so much material can be moved so quickly in the Gulf War, the rich countries can surely learn to move quickly and effectively to deal with famine, whether oil is involved or not. But all good intentions, all generosity, will be completely wasted unless we find a way of dealing with one particular and enormous problem. That problem is the growth of world population.

We have reached the point where spaceship Earth is too overloaded to feed us all. We have to restrict population growth and we have to do it now.

The choice is ours

When we are faced with the evidence of hunger and famine in the world it is easy to feel overwhelmed and helpless. If we allow that to happen then either we start looking for someone else to blame or we do nothing at all. But we do have other choices. We can recognise just how closely we are all connected to the hungry people of the world; we can recognise that their problems are also our problems. When the British entertainer, Lenny Henry, visited Ethiopia he said:

'Going out there changed all my ideas completely. For a start I recognised that each of those starving figures we'd seen on the screen was an individual with the same pride, the same dignity, the same intelligence and the same feeling as you and I.'

Led by him and other comics, the British people raised almost 13 million pounds of aid money on the Day of Comic Relief.

We can also help by taking action to change the attitude and behaviour of our businessmen and politicians. In 1991 the British government cancelled debts of half a billion pounds owed by the poorest countries, some of whom could not even pay the interest on their debts. It is important that we all support such action and encourage politicians to take this more long-sighted view. This kind of help will prove more valuable than temporary support in the form of food handouts. We also need to protest at what is wrong. In the USA public protest over the connection between the beefburger trade and damage being done to Central American environments (see page 24) led to a drastic reduction in that beef trade. Protests continue, and continue to have some effect.

We can all buy presents at the charity shops, we can take part in a fun run, or organise coffee

A foreign aid worker advises local women from a women's agricultural cooperative in Niger, Africa.

mornings and car boot sales to help raise money for relief organisations. We can support the politicians who take up the issues of hunger and famine, and we can fight against the politicians who do not.

We need to keep in touch with the belief that most people do want to help. Workers in a biscuit factory demonstrated recently that they wanted to help Oxfam to deal with the problem of encouraging starving children to eat when they have lost all interest in food. Oxfam developed a high-energy biscuit that was very nutritious: the Oxfam Energy Biscuit (OEB). When trials proved that children would eat the biscuit as a first step away from starvation, Oxfam placed a large order with the company that helped to develop the OEB. An extra shift was set up to produce the biscuits and all the workers donated their entire night's pay to Oxfam.

Such activities are extremely valuable and lead to clear benefits for the hungry. But there is one other and even bigger change we can make that will have the most lasting effect of all. We can change ourselves and how we live. The most important question for us all, adults and children, is do we choose to be part of the problem or part of the solution?

If we all ate less meat, that could become a permanent help. If we shopped more carefully, and if we wasted less, that would help. If, when we set up home with a partner and started a family, we considered carefully just how many children we wanted, that would be a permanent help. We can also stop pretending that each new generation can have a better start in life than the previous one; this will reduce the pressure on world resources coming from developing countries. The truth is that our children's lives will be very different from ours.

GLOSSARY

deforestation – the clearance of all forest from a large area of ground.

donor country – a country giving aid to another country.

environment – what a place is like and how the people live in it.

epidemic – the widespread occurrence of a disease.

famine – complete absence of food

hunger – shortage of food

Infant Mortality Rate (IMR) – the number of babies in every 1000 live births who die before reaching their first birthday

inter-related – one thing being closely linked with another; for example, soil fertility and crop yields.

irrigation – bringing water to the land by artificial methods

malnutrition – a condition caused by lack of the appropriate kinds of food, literally 'bad feeding'. It may occur as the result of hunger, of an unbalanced diet or of overeating.

overcropping – growing too many crops in too short a time on the same piece of land. The worst effects of overcropping usually result from growing the *same* crop too many times.

overgrazing – destroying grazing land by having too many animals on the land, or by keeping a smaller number of animals in the same place for too long.

reafforestation – replanting forest on land that has been deforested.

recipient country – a country accepting aid from a donor country.

salinisation – the increase of harmful salts in the soil which are left behind by the evaporation of irrigation water.

surplus – more than is needed; for example, a wheat surplus in the USA.

sustainable – describes something that can be maintained over a long period of time; for example, a type of farming that can be supported by the local environment.